ISBN 978-1-333-36526-4
PIBN 10495548

This book is a reproduction of an important historical work. Forgotten Books uses
state-of-the-art technology to digitally reconstruct the work, preserving the original format
whilst repairing imperfections present in the aged copy. In rare cases, an imperfection in
the original, such as a blemish or missing page, may be replicated in our edition. We do,
however, repair the vast majority of imperfections successfully; any imperfections that
remain are intentionally left to preserve the state of such historical works.

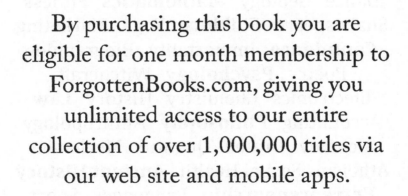

English
Français
Deutsche
Italiano
Español
Português

www.forgottenbooks.com

Mythology Photography **Fiction**
Fishing Christianity **Art** Cooking
Essays Buddhism Freemasonry
Medicine **Biology** Music **Ancient
Egypt** Evolution Carpentry Physics
Dance Geology **Mathematics** Fitness
Shakespeare **Folklore** Yoga Marketing
Confidence Immortality Biographies
Poetry **Psychology** Witchcraft
Electronics Chemistry History **Law**
Accounting **Philosophy** Anthropology
Alchemy Drama Quantum Mechanics
Atheism Sexual Health **Ancient History**
Entrepreneurship Languages Sport
Paleontology Needlework Islam
Metaphysics Investment Archaeology
Parenting Statistics Criminology
Motivational

SETH COOLEY CARY, AUTHOR AND PUBLISHER

JOHN CARY

1755—1823

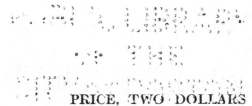

PRICE, TWO DOLLARS

Author and Publisher

REV. SETH C. CARY

DORCHESTER CENTER, BOSTON, MASSACHUSETTS

1908

Publications of Rev. Seth C. Cary

BULLETIN OF THE JOHN CARY DESCENDANTS. *Illustrat*ed. Issued occasionally

THE CARY FAMILY IN ENGLAND. *Illustrat*ed

THE CARY FAMILY IN AMERICA. *Illustrat*ed
> By mail, $5.25 each. Both to one address, $10.00

JOHN AINSWORTH DUNN. For private circulation

THE LATER CARY POEMS. Third Edition. *Illustrated*. Fifty cents each, five
> copies, $2.00

JOHN CARY, 1755-1823. Price, $2.00

In Preparation: JOHN CARY, THE PLYMOUTH PILGRIM: HIS ANCESTRY AND
> DESCENDANTS

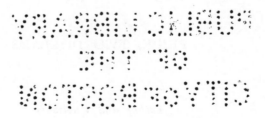
PRESS OF
MURRAY AND EMERY COMPANY
BOSTON, MASS.

PREFACE

Every family has enough of stirring and momentous deeds set to its credit to ennoble it, as well as to enrich history and bless the world.

There is more great history as yet unwritten, that well might serve a useful purpose in the world and lift our thoughts to better things, than now occupies the pages of what we call literature. These actions were performed by those that we call humble, unknown beyond their own small circle.

Human nature has a capacity for greatness, in the midst of many things that are petty, and some that are despicable. Some of these are recorded, but the most are known only to the few, or have already faded out of the memory of those who wrought them.

And yet it is just these that show how rich a field we have in human action and accomplishment. Not all can be recorded; it is only the few that in some strange way find their place in written history, and emphasize the old saw, "As good fish in the sea as ever were caught."

All this is true of the following pages. It is the gathering up of the fragments, of which we would there were more.

So we set down these items, not for egotism but for profit.

SETH C. CARY.

Dorchester Center
Boston, Massachusetts
December, 1908

ILLUSTRATIONS

DEDICATED
TO THE MEMORY OF
MY GRANDPARENTS
JOHN CARY
AND
MARY RUDE
AND THEIR DESCENDANTS

SKETCH OF JOHN CARY

1755–1823

"Your valor we recall,
Your sacrifice, and all
The struggle fierce you made for us and ours."

JOHN CARY, the son of James Cary and Anne Taplin, was born at Kinderhook, Columbia County, New York, February 28, 1755, and baptized in the old Dutch Church, April 23 following, by Pastor Petrus Van Driessen, and Petrus Van Valkenburg and Bata Van Deusen were the sponsors.

His mother's brother was John Taplin, who for ten years was in the French and Indian War, and was doubtless a welcome if not frequent visitor at their home. The military operations were confined in those days largely to the summer and fall months, which gave ample time for them to see him on his journeys to and from Fort William Henry, Crown Point and old Fort "Ti," to his home in Marlboro and Westboro. He rose from sergeant to a lieutenant colonelcy, and King George afterward made him a judge of the Court of Common Pleas.

So this lad had the opportunity of hearing the stories of war, adventure, and the scenes of forest life among the Indians, at first hand. He is now grown to young manhood, and we find him among friends at Preston, Conn., where in April, 1775, he enlists as a private in the company of Captain Ebenezer Witter, "for the relief of Boston in the Lexington Alarm," and served six days. Asher Rude was in the same company.

May 19, 1775, he enlisted again, this time in the 4th Company, Captain Obadiah Johnson, and 3d Regiment, commanded by Colonel Israel Putnam. It is recorded that he was out till December 15, but another account says that three men of this company went with Colonel Benedict Arnold in the expedition to Quebec, and that all returned.

This expedition was one of the most difficult, taxing, and arduous

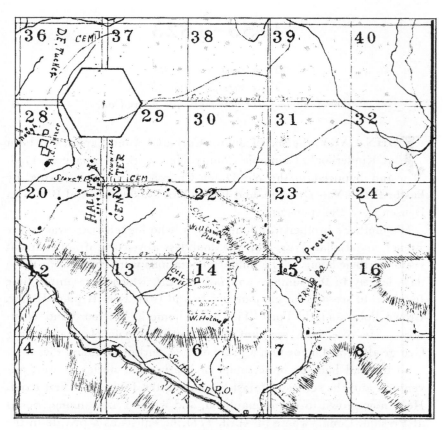

FARMS OF JOHN CARY, HALIFAX, VERMONT
IN LOT NO. 14

experienced by any of our troops during the Revolutionary struggle. It is probable that John Cary was transferred to this command because the Arnolds and Carys had intermarried, or for the reason that his cousin, Timothy Bigelow, was a major under Arnold, or possibly because he was a nephew of Colonel John Taplin.

A recent writer says: "Late in the summer of 1775, Washington despatched a small force under Benedict Arnold, through the Kennebec Valley against Quebec, hoping either to gain possession of the Canadian capital or to aid Schuyler by drawing Carleton to its defence.

The route of Arnold's detachment lay through an unknown wilderness. The march itself was a campaign,—a campaign against the forest and the flood, against fatigue, sickness, and famine. The contest proved close and pitiless, and the issue remained long in doubt. In so keen a struggle, the smallest of circumstances was enough to throw the victory this way or that. Every detail, therefore, not only enlists the attention of the reader, but well repays his interest."—*Professor Justin H. Smith.*

This expedition left Cambridge, September 13, 1775, marching through Medford, Salem, and Ipswich to Newburyport, where they embarked for the Kennebec River. The vessels took them as far as practicable, and then left them with all their supplies of provisions, ammunition, etc., etc., to find their way up an unknown river, through a trackless wilderness, to Quebec more than three hundred miles away. Another writer says: "The troops are now at the mouth of the Kennebec River, and thus far the journey of these brave men has not been an arduous one, but now is about to be commenced a march which for courage, clear grit, boldness, bravery, patience, suffering, endurance and fortitude, under the most trying and at times painful circumstances, stands, we believe, without a parallel in the world's history."—*Ezra D. Hines.*

Bateaux had been provided, and upon these they loaded all this material. But the river was in places shallow, obstructed by rapids and falls, and against all these difficulties they pressed on, encouraged by the hope of success. At these obstructions, the boats were unloaded, the material and boats carried to smooth water above, reloaded, and again they pushed on toward the goal of their hopes—Quebec

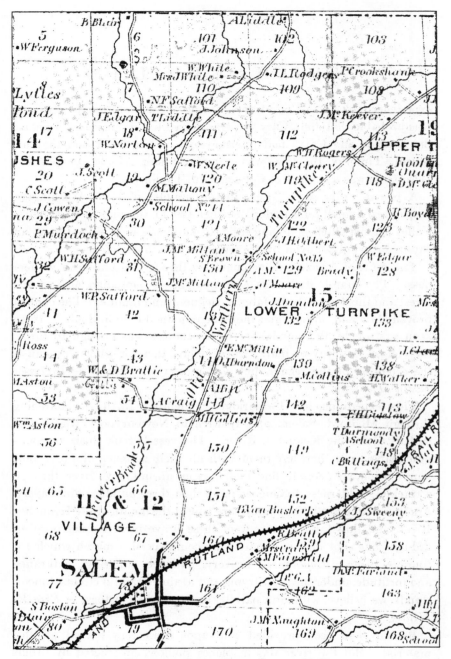

FARMS OF JOHN CARY, SALEM, N. Y.
LOT NO. 109

SKETCH OF HIS LIFE

Many of these carries were long, the banks were in places swampy, but they did not stop, but floundered through swamps, expecting attacks from a wily foe, and amid increasing cold.

Some of the troops returned; game was scarce, and after a time they were put on short allowance, while the work was not lessened, but largely increased; their comrades were falling by the way, or were helped along by great effort. At length their provisions were exhansted, and they ate their oxen, the horses and the dogs; and in their most desperate straits, they boiled their moccasins to secure a little sustenance; but these men did not stop!

Late in October, reaching the sparsely settled country of the French *habitants*, leaving comrades to die or follow later, still pressing on, after weary days the banks of the St. Lawrence were reached at Point Levi, opposite Quebec, only to find new and stronger foes to meet and grapple with. A wide and deep river was in their front, and just beyond this was the strongest fortification on the continent to besiege. And they met both without flinching!

Leaving a guard of sixty men at Point Levi, on the night of November 13 the crossing of the St. Lawrence was made, and in the morning this handful of thinly clad, half-starved patriots made a demonstration against this Gibraltar of the West! Nothing seemed to be able to stop that band of heroes! They were possessed of the combined qualities of Cromwell's men of iron, and the Old Guard of Napoleon!

The town was attacked repeatedly, despite starvation, frozen limbs and blinding storms. Reinforced by Montgomery, a supreme effort was made in the early morning of December 31, 1775. In the midst of a blinding snowstorm, they made their great assault. It was a desperate hand-to-hand struggle, against superior numbers, unknown surroundings, and almost Arctic cold. The close of the conflict found them in a sad plight: Montgomery was dead, Arnold badly wounded, many of the officers and men dead, wounded or prisoners; those who escaped went back to their camp, and took up again the siege, which was kept up in a more or less effective manner during the long, cold winter.

As spring opened and the ice began to break up, there was much anxiety, since they were too weak to make a direct assault, and knew

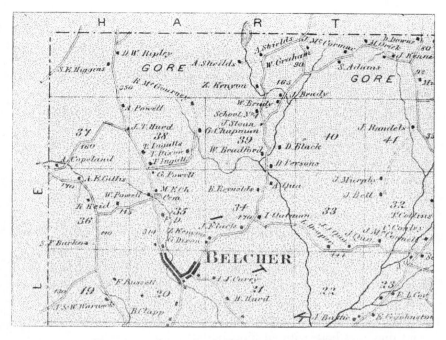

FARMS OF JOHN CARY, BELCHER, NEW YORK
LOTS NOS. 38 AND 21

BIRD'S-EYE VIEW OF THE FARM OF JOHN CARY, BELCHER, NEW YORK
LOT NO. 21

that reinforcements were coming from England, and would come up the river as soon as the ice went out. On the fifth of May, hearing that the British war vessels were near, orders were given to remove the sick to Three Rivers; and on the morning of the sixth, the frigate Surprise and the Isis and Martin appeared, troops were landed, and the Americans were soon hurrying toward Montreal.

The small force at Point Levi, in which, doubtless, was John Cary, moved toward Montreal, on that side of the St. Lawrence, and barely escaped capture by one of the war vessels, which had landed a force for that purpose. But plunging into the forest, they made a wide circuit and after much hardship reached Sorel, at the mouth of the Richelieu, which is the outlet of Lake Champlain. The forces that gathered here remained till late in June; and probably John Cary reached his home at Halifax, Vermont, then in the Province of New York, some time in July. On the twenty-third of September following, he buys a farm adjoining that of his father.

But he is still a patriot and a soldier. For in 1777, in order to secure a living for the family, and possibly also on account of his enfeebled condition resulting from that awful Quebec campaign, he hired a man to go into the army in his place, while he planted a crop. That man was killed at Saratoga.

Hearing, however, in his Green Mountain home of the expected attack of Baum and his Hessians on Bennington, he shouldered his musket and trudged over the mountains, only to be just too late for the battle, but showing his love of liberty.

The Revolutionary struggle is not yet over when John Cary hastens away to Preston, Connecticut, where he enlisted, and where he and Mary Rude unite their fortunes on the twelfth day of November, 1780, Rev. Levi Hart, D.D. (a son-in-law of Dr. Bellamy), officiating. Just how he came to find this good woman, we are not able to say, but remembering that Asher and Oliver Rude were with him in his early army experience, and that he had kindred about there, doubtless this will solve the mystery.

The marriage was a century and a quarter ago, but the wedding trip was up the beautiful Connecticut Valley, and thence up one of its most charming tributaries, the Deerfield River. Here they lived till the birth

----Home of--John Cary, Belcher, New York

Another View

of their first child, Susannah, the parents probably dying soon after. Owing to the almost warlike conditions on the border, between the New Yorkers and the Vermonters, each of whom claimed that territory, or perhaps desiring to extend their wedding trip, they leave the Green Mountains behind them, and locate in the beautiful valley of the Hudson, having doubtless heard of its fertility from their uncle, Colonel John Taplin, who had traversed the valley on his way to and from Lake George, Crown Point, and Fort "Ti"; and also having seen it on his way from Quebec.

Here in Charlotte County, now Washington, they settle down, but not till he has bought a farm in White Creek, now Salem, another just north of Belcher in the town of Hebron, and yet another just east of Belcher, which suits him, and from the original forest he clears up a farm, and rears a family of four sons and four daughters, at least four of whom become school teachers.

When the War of 1812-14 breaks out, he is too old to again enter the service, but he can now do better, so he sends three of his four sons and a son-in-law, all of whom are present or on the way to the battle of Plattsburg, which was fought September 11, 1814.

April 29, 1783, John Cary bought of Alexander Kennedy the north half of lot No. 21, Kempe's Patent, in the district of Black Creek, afterward the town of Hebron, containing one hundred and nineteen acres, for which he paid "one hundred Pounds Current money of the State of New York." The "quit rents" were not discharged till February 7, 1816.

This farm was situated a little east of Belcher, in the westerly part of Hebron. Here John Cary and Mary Rude settled permanently, having now two children. This farm was joined on the east by land of Honorable Alexander Webster, who came from Scotland in 1772; and on the north by the farm of Jonathan Clough.

The town of Hebron was settled about 1769-70, by David Whedon, John Hamilton and Robert Creighton. David Whedon's son David, born in 1771, was the first white child born in the town.

At the time when John Cary brought his little family and settled here permanently, there was no school, and a church was organized not many years after by the Presbyterians; they were miles from a gristmill.

JOHN CARY, 1755-1823

It is probable that not a stick of timber had been cut on this farm when they came. He built a log house near the southwest corner of the farm, and just east of a little brook, and where it crossed the road; a few plum trees in later years marked the garden spot. This house was soon outgrown, and another was built on higher ground, and just west of the present frame house, in what was afterwards known as the "clothes yard." In later years the frame house was built, and compared well with others of the neighborhood.

The boys of the family were kept busy in clearing the original forest and doing the farm work, while the girls, led by the good mother, looked after the house, spun, wove, and made the clothing of the family. There were few books, but so well did the children use what they had, that four at least of the eight became teachers.

John Cary was a God-fearing man, and in later life was baptized by Elder Brown of Hartford. He was a good singer, and the neighbors loved to go to his home and listen to his singing.

After the death of Mary Rude, he married Mrs. Susannah Cary, who survived him some years.

He made his will April 1, 1823, died the following day, and was buried in the burying-ground on the farm.

His will is as follows:

I, John Cary, of the town of Hebron, county of Washington, State of New York, considering the uncertainty of this mortal life, being of sound and perfect mind and memory, blessed be Almighty God for the same!

Do make and publish this as and for my last will and Testament; That is to say, after the payment of all my just debts and funeral charges by my Executors hereafter to be named:

I give and bequeath to my beloved wife Susannah Cary, the use of one third of all my freehold property during her natural life. Also I give and bequeath to the said Susannah one brown cow and one white-faced cow, and one two-year-old heifer. Also all such household furniture and bedding which was formerly hers or has been made while she lived with me. Also the use and occupancy of the north room and bedroom adjoining in my now dwelling house, with a privilege in t kitchen and cellar during her lifetime.

1. I give to my sons in the following manner, viz., to my son James Cary two dollars besides what he has heretofore received.

[18]

2. I give to my son Isaac Cary two dollars besides what he has heretofore received.

3. I give to my son George Cary my three-year-old horse and saddle.

4. I give and bequeath to my son John Cary, Jun., all my freehold and personal property which shall not otherwise be disposed of on this condition, viz., that he shall furnish good and sufficient maintenance for my daughter Mary Cary as long as she remains unmarried. Also that he furnish good and sufficient maintenance for my daughter Susannah Cary whenever she shall become unable to maintain herself as long as she remains unmarried.

5. I give and bequeath to my daughters Susannah Cary and Mary Cary all the household furniture and bedding and clothing which formerly belonged to their Mother (excepting thereout one bed), to be divided equally between them.

6. I give and bequeath to my daughter Catherine Liddle one certain note of hand against George Liddle for twenty dollars dated 21st Dec'r 1816, together with the sum of one dollar.

7. I give and bequeath to my daughter Olive Barton two dollars besides what she has heretofore received.

Lastly. I do hereby constitute and appoint my son John Cary and Abel Wood Executors of this my last will and testament hereby revoking and disallowing all other and former wills and testaments heretofore by me made: In witness whereof, I, the said John Cary have to my last will and testament set my hand and seal this first day of April in the year of our lord one thousand eight hundred and twenty-three.

(Signed) John Cary. [L.S.]

Signed sealed and published by the testator
as his last will and testament in the
presence of
    Israel McConnell
    Thomas Gourlay
    Elijah Clough

VIEW OF QUEBEC 1759

COAT OF ARMS OF SIR JOHN CARY
CHIEF BARON OF THE EXCHEQUER UNDER RICHARD II.
From The Cary Family in England, by permission

COAT OF ARMS OF SIR ROBERT CARY, KNIGHT
GIVEN HIM BY KING HENRY V.
From The Cary Family in England, by permission

THE
ANCESTRY OF JOHN CARY
1755—1823

COMPILED BY THE LATE PROF. HENRY G. CARY, BOSTON

I.

ADAM DE KARI was born about 1170 and, according to the Domesday Book, was Lord of Castle Kari, Somersetshire, in 1198. The town is now called Castle Cary. He married Ann, daughter of Sir William Trevett, Knight.

II.

JOHN DE KARY was born about 1200, and married Elizabeth, daughter of Sir Richard Stapleton, Knight.

III.

WILLIAM DE KARY was born about 1230, and married Alice, the daughter of Sir William Beaumont, Knight.

IV.

JOHN DE KARRY was born about 1270, and married Phillippa, daughter of Sir Warren Archdeacon, Knight.

V.

SIR WILLIAM CARY was born about 1300, and married Margaret Bozume of Clovelly. The spelling of the name was changed during the reign of Edward II. and has since been spelled Cary.

VI.

SIR JOHN CARY, KNIGHT, was born 1325; married Agnes, daughter of Lord Stafford. No issue. After her death he married Jane. daughter of Sir Guy de Brien, Knight.

VII.

SIR JOHN CARY, KNIGHT, was born in Devonshire, in 1350; on the fifth of November, 1387, King Richard II. made him Judge and Chief Baron of the Exchequer.

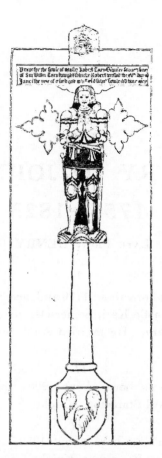

Prayr for the foule of Maifter Robert Cary Efquier fumtyme hie of Sir Willm Cary knyght Which Robert deceffid the xvth day of June i the yere of lord god m vc xl ... fowle ihu haue mercy

TOMB OF SIR ROBERT CARY, CLOVELLY

Married Margaret Holway, and owned Cockington and Clovelly, which he bought in 1390.

He was banished to Waterford, Ireland, after Richard II. was put to death by Henry IV. He was four years in banishment, and died in 1404.

VIII.

SIR ROBERT CARY, KNIGHT. married Elizabeth, daughter of Philip Courtenay, Knight. She died leaving no issue, and he married Jane, daughter of Sir William Hanchford, Knight.

He defeated the Knight of Aragon at Smithfield, London, and thus upheld the honor of England. For this King Henry V. presented him a coat of arms, and restored to him Clovelly.

THE STORY OF THE CARY COAT OF ARMS
AS TOLD BY OLD CHRONICLERS

"In the beginning of the reign of Henry V. (1413-1422) a certain Knight-errant of Aragon, having passed through divers countries, and performed many feats of Arms, arrived here in England, where he challenged any man of his rank and quality to make a trial of his skill in arms. This challenge was accepted by Sir Robert Cary, between whom a cruel encounter, and a long and doubtful combat was waged in Smithfield, London. But at length this noble Champion vanquished the presumptuous Aragonois, for which King Henry V. restored unto him a good part of his father's lands, which for his loyalty to Richard II. he had been deprived of by Henry IV. and authorized him to bear the Arms of a Knight of Aragon, which the noble posterity continue to wear unto this day; for according to the laws of Heraldry, whoever fairly in the field conquers his adversary may justify the wearing of his Arms."—*Burke's Heraldry.*

Another account is so quaint that it is placed before the reader:

"In the time of Henry V. cam out of Aragon a lusty gentleman into England, and challenged to do feites of armes, with any English gentleman without exception. This Sir Robert Cary hearing thereof, made suit forthwith to the Prince, that he might answer the challenge, which was granted. and Smithfield was the place appointed for the same, who, at the day and time prefixed, both parties mett and did performe

THE PIER, CLOVELLY

CLOVELLY, HIGH STREET

sundrie feates of armes, but in the end this Robert gave the foils and overthrow to the Aragon Knight, disarmed and spoiled him, which his doinge so well pleased the Prince, that he receyved him into great favor, caused him to be restored to the most part of his father's landes, and willed him also for a perpetuall memorie of his victorie, that he should henceforth give the same armes as the Aragon Knight, which is Argent, on bend sable three roses argent for before they did beare gules, chevron entre, three swans argent."—*Herald's Visitation*, 1620.

IX.

SIR PHILIP CARY, KNIGHT, was born in 1400, married Christian Orchard, and died in 1437.

X.

SIR WILLIAM CARY, KNIGHT OF COCKINGTON, was born 1437; married Elizabeth Paulett. At the battle of Tewkesbury in the War of the Roses, he took sanctuary in the church, but was betrayed, beheaded, and his property confiscated.

From Sir William Cary's son Thomas, born 1465, descended the three lines of nobility:

1. Baron Hunsdon.
2. The Earl of Monmouth.
3. Viscount Falkland.

From his son Robert, born 1460, descended the families of

1. Clovelly.
2. Torre Abbey.
3. Somersetshire.

XI.

SIR ROBERT CARY was born in 1460 and died in 1540; inherited Clovelly from his father, or restored by King Henry VII. Married first, Jane Carew, daughter of the Baron of Castle Carew; second, Agnes, daughter of Sir William Hody, Knight and Chief Baron of the Exchequer under Henry VII.; third, Margaret Fulkeram.

His tomb with inscription is in the Clovelly Church.

XII.

WILLIAM CARY was born in 1500, and died in 1572. In 1532, in the reign of King Henry VIII., he was sheriff of Bristol, Somerset, and was afterward mayor.

MANOR HOUSE, CASTLE CARY. KING CHARLES II., AFTER HIS DEFEAT
BY CROMWELL AT THE BATTLE OF WORCESTER, SLEPT
IN THIS HOUSE, SEPTEMBER 16, 1651

KENILWORTH CASTLE. ONE OF THE HOMES OF THE CARYS

CLOVELLY COURT. THE HOME OF THE CARYS

CLOVELLY. VIEW FROM THE HOBBY DRIVE

HIS ANCESTRY

XIII.

ROBERT CARY was born in 1525, at Bristol, and died in 1570.

XIV.

WILLIAM CARY was born in 1560; was sheriff of Bristol in 1599; mayor of Bristol in 1611. He had eight sons, three of whom came to America in 1634, 1635 and 1640.

XV.

JOHN CARY was born near Bristol, England, about 1610. He came to America in 1634, landing at Plymouth, but soon made his home in Duxbury. Here he owned a farm, and tradition says became the first Latin teacher in the Plymouth Colony.

He married Elizabeth, daughter of Francis Godfrey. About 1650 he became an original proprietor in the Duxbury New Plantation, and at its organization as the town of Bridgewater, in 1656, was elected constable, the only officer elected that year. He was already the clerk of the Land Company. He was afterward elected town clerk, and held the office till his death in 1681.

His farm, which was in what is now West Bridgewater, was a mile wide and seven miles long. He was a good man, and highly respected in the Colony. He reared a family of twelve children.

XVI.

JOHN CARY was born in Duxbury in 1645; married Abigail, daughter of Samuel Allen, and reared a family of eleven children.

In 1680 he became an original proprietor of Bristol, where he became deacon of the church, town and county clerk, and where he died.

XVII.

JAMES CARY was born in Bridgewater, in 1680, and was one of the youngest who emigrated to Bristol.

He removed to Newport, where he married Bridget, daughter of John Pococke, Attorney General of Rhode Island.

XVIII.

JAMES CARY was born in Newport, in 1728; served in the English navy. Became a tanner by trade; married Anne Taplin, whose

CLOVELLY. INTERIOR OF CHURCH, SHOWING CARY TABLETS

THE JOHN CARY MONUMENT. ERECTED ON THE OLD HOMESTEAD
WEST BRIDGEWATER, MASSACHUSETTS, 1905

NEAR THIS SPOT WAS THE HOME OF

JOHN CARY.

BORN IN SOMERSETSHIRE, ENGLAND,
HE BECAME IN 1651 AN ORIGINAL PROPRIETOR,
AND HONORED SETTLER ON THIS RIVER.
WAS CLERK OF THE PLANTATION.
WHEN THE TOWN OF BRIGEWATER WAS
INCORPORATED, IN 1656, HE WAS ELECTED
CONSTABLE, THE FIRST AND ONLY OFFICER OF
THAT YEAR.
WAS TOWN CLERK UNTIL HIS DEATH IN 1681.
TRADITION SAYS,
HE WAS THE FIRST TEACHER OF LATIN IN
PLYMOUTH COLONY.
THIS TABLET IS ERECTED BY HIS DESCENDANTS
IN MEMORY
OF THEIR HISTORIC AND NOBLE ANCESTOR.

BRONZE TABLET ON MONUMENT

JOHN CARY, 1755-1823

brother was a lieutenant colonel in the French and Indian War, and afterward judge of the Court of Common Pleas.

He owned land in Middletown, Connecticut, and also in Marlboro and Halifax, Vermont.

XIX.

JOHN CARY (see special sketch).

Children:

1.

Susannah, b. in Halifax, Vt., 1781; never married; a bright and intelligent woman, and a school teacher. Lived with her brother George at Castile, N. Y., where she died in 1847.

2.

James, b. in White Creek, Charlotte County, N. Y., later called Salem, Washington County, N. Y. He taught school in his youth; was a soldier in the War of 1812-14, and was engaged in the battle of Plattsburg; removed to North Creek, Warren County, N. Y., and died there May 6, 1865. He was a sincere Christian and a member of the Methodist Episcopal Church. He married Abigail Leonard (b. May 21, 1790, d. Mar. 23, 1874).

Children:

1. Nathaniel, who went to Spartansburg, Pa.
2. Thomas, who went to Westfield, N. Y.
3. John, b. Aug. 25, 1813; m. and reared a family at North Creek and d. there July 26, 1872.
4. Alvin, b. Dec. 11, 1814; m. Mary A. ——— and lived and died at North Creek.
5. George was a soldier in the Civil War, and removed to French Creek, N. Y.
6. Patty, b. June 4, 1820; m. Mr. Humes at North Creek, and had Olive who m. George Griswold of Pottersville; Emeline, who m. Mortimer Tyrrell; Mary Ann and Lilly.
7. Polly, b. 1824 and lived at North Creek.

3.

Catherine, b. at Belcher, 1785; m. George Liddle and d. at Johnsburg, May 29, 1865.

HIS DESCENDANTS

Children:
1. Mary.
2. Olive, m. John Ward, a Baptist preacher, and had two sons and two daughters.
3. Rachel, m. Isaac Morehouse and had seven children.
4. John.
5. George.

4.

Isaac, b. Belcher, Aug. 27, 1787; m. Anne Barton (b. Aug. 26, 1786; d. in Chicago, Mar. 20, 1864; buried in Erie, Pa.), July 29, 1810; he d. at Mt. Clemens, Mich., Aug. 24, 1830.   They lived in Minerva and Troy, N. Y.   He was a soldier in the War of 1812-14, and was in the Battle of Plattsburg.

Children:
1. Harvey, b. July 11, 1811; m. Jane Russell, and had:
   (1) Isaac.
   (2) Anne Jane.
   (3) Edward.
   (4) Eliza.
   (5) Ella.
   (6) Harvey.
   (7) Warren.
   (8) Albert.
   (9) Clara.
   (10) Ida.
   (11) John.
   (12) Alice.

Five of these sons became railway men, and attained distinction.
2. Phebe, b. June 8, 1813; m. Mr. Rice, and had George, a musician in the Civil War, who died in the service.
3. Jane, b. Mar. 22, 1815; m. Dea. Daniel E. Ambrose (Co. A. 19th Ill.; d. June, 1886); she d. Nov. 1893.
4. James Warren, b. April 24, 1818; lived at Troy, and Rome, N. Y., where he d. Feb. 15, 1903; m. ███, Mary Ann Vanderburg, and had Ella, who m. Arthur Mengel; ███ ████ and had:

JOHN CARY, 1755-1823

(1) Warren W.
(2) Harley E.
(3) Nettie R.
(4) Lila M.
(5) Fayette R.

5. Daniel Barton, b. April 23, 1820; m. Elizabeth Schaffer, who d. at Lake Forrest, Ill., Dec., 1897; he d. Feb. 21, 1898.
Children:

    (1) Charles.

    (2) Mary Elizabeth.

    (3) Delia, b. Dec., 1849; m. John Bowers, 1871.

    (4) Jane, b. June 11, 1852; d. 1871.

    (5) Martha Washington, b. Feb. 22, 1855; m. Julius Knox, Feb. 22, 1872, and had:

        1. Elizabeth, b. Dec. 7, 1873; m. James Matson, Oct. 12, 1893.

        2. Wilhimena, b. April 9, 1874; m. Goetleib Michael Liedke.

        3. George Edward, b. Dec. 10, 1876; m. Elizabeth Heiple, Nov. 1894, who d. May 12, 1895; m. second, Ida Wickousen, Feb. 1, 1899.

        4. Julius Frederick, b. May 2, 1878; m. Catherine Meyer, Sept. 19, 1907.

        5. William C., b. Dec. 18, 1880; d. Jan. 1, 1881.

        6. Alexander Daniel, b. Nov. 20, 1881; m. Katherine Wagstaff, April 3, 1906.

        7. Martha Francis, b. Sept. 20, 1883; m. Henry Sherer, Feb. 22, 1903.

        8. Eva Irene, b. Feb. 11, 1889; m. Albert Boelke, June 19, 1907.

        9. Clarence Harvey, b. Feb. 9, 1891.

        10. Crystal Delia, b. Feb. 9, 1891.

        11. Dorothy Amelie, b. May 31, 1897.

    (6) Jesse, b. Jan., 1856; d. in infancy.

    (7) Alice, b. Mar. 21, 1858; m. Andrew Schaffer, Oct. 1873, and had:

HIS DESCENDANTS

1. Charles, b. Nov. 16, 1874; m. Gertrude Mc-Cormick, May, 1892.
2. Sylvester, b. 1876, d. in infancy.
3. Alice, b. Oct., 1879; m. John Vaughn, 1896. The mother died Oct. 18, 1881.

(8) Daniel Isaac, b. Troy, N. Y., Dec. 21, 1860; m. Wilhamena Weinburg June, 1888, and has several children.

(9) Harvey, b. Feb. 14, 1832: m. Laura ———, 1890, Mexico, Tex.

(10) Warren, b. Feb. 14, 1862; d. 1871.

(11) Carl, b. April 7, 1838; m. Ella Arnold, 1891, Waco, Tex.

6. Clarissa Olive, b. May 22, 1824, Troy, N. Y.; m. Alexander Adolph Bilinski, Feb. 4, 1857. Count Alexander Adolph Bilinski was born in the village of Borsuki, near Balta, Province of Podalia, Poland, Jan. 1, 1814. He took part in the Polish Revolution of 1830-32, was taken prisoner and after many months' confinement in an Austrian prison, he was given the choice of death, or exile to Siberia or America. Choosing the latter, he landed in New York in 1833. In 1834 he entered the United States military service at the arsenal in Troy, N. Y., where he remained six years, rising to the rank of orderly sergeant; was many times detailed to work requiring great bravery, and performed the same with honor. He resigned his position in 1840, and removed to Waukegan, Ill. In 1849 he made the overland trip to California; returning to Illinois two years later, he settled at Diamond Lake, where he resided till his death, Aug. 13, 1886.

Children:

(1) Jennie Clara, b. May 28, 1858; m. John A. Singer, Nov. 1, 1876, and had:
1. Jean Etta, b. Feb. 1, 1878.
2. Merritt Alexander, b. Jan. 19, 1880; m. Lillian M. Arentz, Aug. 25, 1901, and had Jean Eleanor, June 6, 1902; m. second, Clair D. Vallette, April 14, 1883.

Mrs. Clarissa Olive (Cary) Bilinski

HIS DESCENDANTS

(2) Annah Olive, b. Dec. 25, 1859; m. George N.
Gridley, Sept. 27, 1883, and had:
1. Maud, b. Oct. 6, 1886.
2. Amy Belle, b. Sept. 21, 1888.

5.

Olive Cary, b. April 29, 1789; m. Simon Barton, and d. July 22, 1867;
moved to Moriah, N. Y., about 1820.

Children:
1. William Adams, b. Bennington, Vt., Jan. 11, 1808, and d.
at Crown Point, N. Y., Jan. 1897; m. Electa Taylor and
had eight children.
2. Lyman, M.D., b. Sept. 19, 1812, Belcher, N. Y.; d. at
Willsboro, N. Y., Oct. 20, 1899; m. Minerva Aikin, and
at his death left five children:
(1) William G., M.D.
(2) Mrs. William Keefe.
(3) Mrs. B. J. Chatterton.
(4) Susannah Chase, wife of George A. Perry, New
York, who had:
1. Ralph Barton, professor at Harvard, b. July
3, 1876; m. Rachel Berenson, b. 1880, Boston;
and had Ralph Barton, Jr., Sept. 29, 1906.
2. Edward De Wolf, b. Oct. 2, 1880.
(5) Mrs. Kenneth Laurie.

6.

Mary, b. 1791, and never married. She was an invalid and lived
with her brother John on the old farm. She was familiarly called
"Aunt Molly," and was a student of the Bible. Died July 18, 1849.

7.

John; see special sketch.

8.

George, b. 1799, at Belcher, and d. at Castile, N. Y., 1844; was a
school teacher and something of a musician; m. Adaline Burlingham
who d. in 1866.

SUSANNAH (CARY) GOULD

ANNA COOLEY (CARY) MERITHEW

JOHN CARY, 1755-1823

Children:

1. Benjamin, familiarly called "Ben," b. 1828; m. Miss Marks, and had Adaline, b. 1865; William Norman, who d. at the age of fifteen. Their home is at Galesburg, Ill.

2. John, b. 1830; m. Mary A. Fish, Feb. 22, 1855, and had:

    (1) Addie B. who m. Thomas H. Sutherland, Feb. 5, 1880, and had Frank and Harry J.; she d. April 24 1897, and he d. June 30, following.

    (2) Alice M., m. William Burridge, Dec. 30, 1886.

    (3) Ida F., m. H. W. Allen, Rockford, Ill.

John Cary lived on the old farm at Castile, N. Y., and d. Dec. 23, 1906. The two brothers, aged seventy-six and seventy-eight, visited friends in Boston in 1905.

XX.

JOHN CARY, 1793–1865.

He was born at Belcher, New York, September 2, on the old farm, bought by his father in 1783. His boyhood and youth were spent in clearing up this farm, together with the usual work that comes to the sons of pioneers. Conditions were narrow, but intelligent parents and fraternal love made the most of them.

In the War of 1812-14, he was a private in the West Hebron company, which was attached to the Hebron and Salem regiment. In the campaign of Plattsburg, his company, on the day of the battle, was on a slow-going sloop, on the way to Plattsburg, but was not engaged. In after years, he received for this service a land warrant for one hundred and sixty acres of land, from the United States Government.

In 1815, he bought of John Hornby a farm of one hundred and ten acres in Perry, Genesee County, New York, which after the division became Wyoming County; in 1822 this was sold to his brother George, and he returned to care for his father. The home farm came to him by will.

The winter of 1815-16 was spent in teaching school in the home district. In the State militia he became a sergeant in 1816, and an ensign in 1817. Like his ancestor, John Cary, he was elected constable of the town of Hebron in 1820-21.

January 9, 1823, he married Catherine, daughter of Seth and Anne

Isaac J. Cary

(Smith) Cooley, of Salem, New York, who was a descendant, in the sixth generation, from Benjamin Cooley, who in 1646, at the age of twenty-four, was a selectman of Springfield, Massachusetts. There were six children who lived to be married.

Children:

1. Matthew, b. Dec. 28, 1823; d. Nov. 24, 1824.

2. Susannah, b. Sept. 2, 1825; m. John Gould, Jan. 1, 1852, and had Kate S., April 7, 1853; the mother died Jan. 14, 1854, and Katie was brought up in the old home; she m. Selden O. Swain, April 13, 1879, and had:

    (1) Blanche Cramer, b. Mar. 29, 1880, and m. Bert G. Rees, Jan. 17, 1906.

    (2) Charles R., b. May 4, 1883; d. July 3, 1897.

   Their home is in Creston, Ill.

3. Anna Cooley, b. May 2, 1829; m. Joseph Merithew (b. Dec. 8, 1823; d. Apr. 4, 1902), Nov. 8, 1854, and had:

    (1) Ira J., b. Sept. 18, 1857; m. Emma Northrup, Dec 25, 1883, and had:

        1. E. Northrup, b. May 20, 1886.

        2. Mabel E., b. July 3, 1890.

    (2) Hiram Rogers, b. Dec. 11, 1859.

    (3) Edward S., b. Dec. 18, 1861; m. Annis L. Haynes, Sept. 1, 1897, and had:

        1. Grace Geneva, b. Aug. 9, 1898.

        2. Clifford Harry, b. April 29, 1901.

    (4) Sarah Jennie, b. June 8, 1868; m. Charles Chapman, and had:

        1. Valeta A., b. June 28, 1892.

        2. John J., b. Aug. 28, 1895.

4. Isaac J. b. Aug. 15, 1831: m. first, Martha J. Donaldson, Jan. 1, 1856, and had Henrietta, who died Oct. 3, 1874: the mother died Sept. 27, 1858; m. second, Mary Graham, Jan. 1, 1861, and had:

    (1) John Graham, b. Feb. 14, 1862; m. A. Bell Farwell, Nov. 11, 1885, and had:

        1. Anna Graham, b. July 10, 1890.

CLARINDA BLISS (CARY) COY

JOHN CARY, 1755-1823

2. Ray, who died in infancy.

3. Mary Farwell, b. Mar. 16, 1894.

(2) Samuel Robert, b. May 25, 1863; m. Margaret Dinning, Nov. 19, 1902, and had Marion, April 19, 1904.

In April, 1858, Isaac bought the old farm of his father, and in 1863 built a house for his parents in the "Orchard," where they lived till the death of his father in 1865. Isaac died December 13, 1868.

5. Mary Jane, b. Dec. 10, 1834; m. William Day, Jan. 15, 1856; d. May 31, 1857.

6. Clarinda Bliss, b. Feb. 14, 1836; m. Edward L. Coy, Sept. 21, 1858, and had:

(1) Charles Herbert, b. July 26, 1859; m. Amelia S. Madison, Dec. 27, 1882, and had Howard Winfield.

(2) Seth Willard, M.D., b. May 28, 1863; m. Grace May Capen, Mar. 17, 1892, and had:

1. Edward L., b. Jan. 25, 1894.

2. Ralph, b. Oct. 31, 1899.

(3) Ida Belle, b. Sept. 13, 1865; m. James B. Sievwright, June 19, 1889, and had:

1. Ruth, b. Feb. 3, 1891.

2. Clara May, b. May 3, 1898.

(4) Mabel, b. Aug. 28, 1873; d. Jan. 10, 1895.

Mr. and Mrs. Edward L. Coy have just observed their golden wedding, at Melrose, Massachusetts.

XXI.
Seth Cooley Cary.

He was born at Belcher, N. Y., June 1, 1838, in the old homestead that sheltered four generations of Carys. As a farmer's boy the usual work and experience fell to his lot. The school advantages were of the ordinary character, with chores and work taking precedence in summer, and filling up the winter term with study and work combined.

In 1854-5, he spent the winter term at the Argyle Academy, under the direction of Mr. and Mrs. J. S. Dobbin.

The two following winters were spent at the West Hebron Classical School, which was under the care of **Mr. George D. Stewart.**

Acceding to the request of some of the families, he ventured to teach the district school in the Stewart and Dunham district, in Argyle, in 1857-8.

The next winter he was invited to teach in the home district at Belcher. During a revival of religion in the Methodist Episcopal Church he was converted, December 31, 1858, was baptized soon after, and received on probation, and in July following was taken into full connection. This was in the pastorate of the Rev. John M. Webster, of the Troy Conference.

Feeling the great need of further study, he entered the Troy Conference Academy, at Poultney, Vermont, in the spring of 1859, and with the exception of one term, remained there till June, 1861, being, it was understood, ready for college.

On the day the news was received that Fort Sumter had been fired upon, the students of T. C. A. formed a Cadet Corps, and drilled during the term. Various marches were taken, one extending as far as Middletown, Vermont.

In September, 1861, about the time he had hoped to go to college at Wesleyan University, he had a very severe attack of typhoid fever. The following January he was invited to teach a short term in the Hudson River Academy at Fort Miller, New York.

President Lincoln having called for "three hundred thousand more" troops, he felt impelled to enter the service. Washington County was to raise a regiment of infantry, and he offered to assist the town committee in recruiting the men needed. The committee and townspeople seemed pleased with the work, and he was commissioned a second lieutenant in Company E., 123d Regiment New York Infantry Volunteers. The regiment was organized at Camp Washington, Salem, and they started for the front September 5, 1862. They became a part of the Army of the Potomac, and were engaged in the campaigns of Chancellorsville and Gettysburg.

In September, 1863, after the battle of Chickamauga, the 11th and 12th Corps were sent to help the army near Chattanooga. The ~~123d~~ *1234* New York was at that time in the 1st Brigade, 1st Division, 12th Corps.

JOHN CARY, 1755-1823

Leaving Brandy Station, Virginia, these troops went via Washington, Harpers Ferry, Louisville, Nashville, Tennessee, and the 123d New York spent the fall at Bridgeport, Alabama. The winter was passed at Elk River and near by.

The campaign of Atlanta was begun April 28, 1864, and work and fighting were continuous till Atlanta was taken in September. T` principal actions in which they were engaged were: Resaca, Cassville. Dallas, Lost Mountain, Pine Hill, Kennesaw, Kolb's Farm, Chattahoochee River, Peach Tree Creek. At the last-named battle, July 20, 1864, he was severely wounded in the left leg, from which he ever after suffered.

He was given a leave of absence, but on his return to the Officers' Hospital at Nashville, Tennessee, he was put on special duty by General Thomas. This embraced service on the Board of Claims, a military court martial, and a military commission.

In April, 1865, Richmond having been taken, and General Lee having surrendered at Appomattox, he was relieved of duty at Nashville, and was mustered out with his regiment at Washington, D. C., June 8, 1865, with the rank of adjutant, having been twice promoted in the field.

Still feeling the call to preach, he left in September for Concord, New Hampshire, and entered the Methodist General Biblical Institute, to fit himself for his new calling. But his father died in a few weeks, and he came home to care for the family.

In September, 1866, he went back to Concord, and in June, 1869, graduated from what has since become the School of Theology of Boston University.

In April, 1868, he was invited to become the assistant pastor of Bromfield Street Methodist Episcopal Church, Boston, with Rev. Luther T. Townsend. For two years these very pleasant and congenial relations continued, when the trustees of the University declined further to allow the professors taking charges in the Conference, and both were relieved from this most agreeable work.

Having completed his theological course, he joined the New England Conference in April, 1870, and has served as follows: South Framingham, Jamaica Plain (Boston), Gardner, West Warren, Whitinsville,

KNIBLOE BOUTON CARY

JOHN CARY, 1755-1823

Beverly, Graniteville,—two months only on account of illness,—Winthrop, Maplewood (Malden), Mattapan (Boston), Gardner, Reading, Wollaston (Quincy), Parkman Street (Boston), Egleston Square (Boston), Winchendon. He built churches at Gardner and West Warren, and rebuilt the churches at Maplewood and Wollaston

In 1884 he visited Europe, and a few years later carried to succes completion the erection of a four-thousand-dollar monument for m regiment on Culp's Hill, Gettysburg, being the chairman of the committee. This work required four years of time, and ten thousand miles of travel.

For twenty years he was on the statistical committee of his Conference; president of the Alpha Chapter, Boston University, ten years; biographical secretary of the same since 1896; elected visitor to the School of Theology for four years, by the Alpha Chapter; instructor in the Deaconess Training School since 1896; commandant of the Veterans' Association of the New England Conference since 1896.

For some years he has been interested in the subject of genealogy, and since 1902 has been president of The John Cary Descendants; has been editor of their Bulletin; published The Cary Family in England, Illustrated, in 1906, and The Cary Family in America, Illustrated, in 1907; also two editions of The Cary Poem, the last in 1908; also for private circulation The Genealogy of John Ainsworth Dunn.

He married, first, Mrs. Sarah (Wing) Bouton, October 7, 1873; she died September 21, 1875; married second, Miss Hattie Landon Bouton, April 17, 1878, and had Knibloe Bouton, March 26, 1882; the mother died April 13, 1882; he married third, Jennie Sophia Dunn, M.D., November 20, 1895.

XXII.

KNIBLOE BOUTON CARY.

Born at Beverly, Mass., March 26, 1882; graduated at Gardner High School, 1898; at the Boston Latin School, 1899; at Boston University, 1903.

Entered the employ of the John A. Dunn Company, Gardner, Mass., July, 1903.

SD - #0126 - 290124 - C0 - 229/152/3 - PB - 9781333365264 - Gloss Lamination